Maybe Love

Amanda Currier

Presentation by *BookLeaf Publishing*

Web: www.bookleafpub.com

E-mail: info@bookleafpub.com

ISBN: 9789357443166

First edition 2023

To D...who taught me that it's my life to define as I wish and that because I always have, doesn't mean I always have to. Thank you for reminding me what it feels like to laugh until your muscles ache, for supporting me through one of the hardest times in my life, and for loving me exactly where I was at, no matter what. Thank you for reminding me to enjoy the little things in life. I'm eternally grateful to have found such an amazing ally in such an unlikely place.

ACKNOWLEDGEMENT

I never would've gotten through this year without so many of you, but most of all to my kids. Austin, Alexys, Noah, and Jacob, you gave me a reason to push through when I desperately wanted to give up. You also taught me that Crocs are not acceptable footwear for a night out on the town. And then laughed knowingly when I wore them anyways. I love you guys more than you'll ever know.

PREFACE

In 2022, my life changed abruptly and I had to forge en entirely new path for what my life would look like. What followed was a year of growth, rebirth, and finally becoming comfortable in my own skin for what I ultimately realized was the first time in my life.

Maybe Love

Love is a tidal wave.
Ferocious.
Unstoppable.
It knocks you off your feet
and steals the breath from your lungs.

Love is a January blizzard.
Formidable.
Encompassing.
Blindingly beautiful, crisp and clean,
it belies its potential to bury you alive.

Love is a wildfire.
Unforgiving.
Enveloping.
With a brilliance so surreal,
you fail to notice that it can burn your soul to
ashes.

Or…maybe it isn't.

Maybe the butterflies are an omen.
Maybe the fiery passion is a lethal flame.
Maybe the fireworks are warning shots.

Maybe, just maybe

Love is a sunset.
Humble.
Unwavering.
So quietly, dependably present
that you fail to appreciate its extraordinary
beauty.

Love is a spring rain.
Tender.
Restoring.
Nourishing the thirsty soil,
allowing the dormant flowers a chance to bloom.

Love is a quiet melody.
Peaceful.
Captivating.
One you find yourself humming aloud
with a smile on your lips and peace in your soul.

Maybe love

Sneaks in like the morning sun through the
blinds,
bathing you in the warmth of its glow
long before you even notice it's magnificence.

Somebody's Little Boy

With tattered rags for clothing,
holes in his shoes
and withering hope for his next meal,
he sleeps with vigilant ears

In a perfect display of ignorance
a finely clad man scoffs and shuffles past.
A lady crosses the street with her children
to avoid imagined danger

Unaccompanied children in the park
throw rocks and laugh
at the man who used to be
somebody's little boy.

Beautifully Dangerous

The most beautiful places are usually the most
dangerous

And I know they meant
Mountains
And jungles
And canyon ravines

But the most beautiful place

Being in love

Is exponentially more dangerous
Because it won't kill you

It'll just make you wish it had

the longest night

glancing across the sterile room
she watches
as a piece of her heart
beats outside her body

he's battered and worn
the world is too heavy
too hard
too cold
too unforgiving
for a soul as sweet as his

his pain is palpable
she feels it in every inch of her skin

his sadness is contagious
she is weighed down by his pain
hoping that maybe she can absorb
just a bit of it
just enough to ease the pressure
on his precious heart
and allow him to once again breathe
the innocent, unburdened breath
of childhood

soon she'll have to leave
alone
and leave behind the light
that is her child
in hopes that he can find
the peace his soul deserves

but how do you leave
the best thing you've ever known
in the hands of someone
who doesn't understand
his joy
his light
or the way your heart lights up
when you see him smile

how do you trust
someone who has never seen
the way he loves the world
that tries so hard to break him
to be the ones who bring the light
back into his eyes?

hard things

hard things
come before good things
they say
but sometimes I wonder
how many
hard things must come
before the good

how many heartbreaks
that leave me breathless
and shaking
with boot prints on my heart
before someone
doesn't

how many tears
will I cry
in the dark
in the shower
or into my pillow
before someone
won't

how many nights
will I lay awake

wondering why I'm not enough
not what they needed
not what they wanted
before
I am

how much hard
how much soul crushing
heart breaking
devastatingly
hard
must I endure
before

the good

The Final Goodbye

When I heard that my father died
I knew I had to grieve the loss of him

But how do you grieve for a man you've lost a
hundred times?

How do you say goodbye
to someone you've said goodbye to time after
time after time?

What's left to say besides

Finally.

Finally, the goodbyes are over
I can close that door to my heart
knowing he can't come knocking
asking to be let back in

Finally, I can make peace with the goodbye
knowing I did everything I could
more than I needed to
more than I should have
more than he ever did

He's gone
again
but this time it's different
because for the first time
he did not choose to leave
this time he didn't choose to walk away
from the one person who fought for him her
entire life

Finally, I don't have to wonder
if I caused this goodbye
if I led us here
if I could done more
said more
tried harder

So I will bid him farewell
one last time
and maybe
just maybe
we can both finally find some peace

The Guard

There are walls around his heart
He stands atop them
A hundred arrows in his quiver
and one in his bow
Aimed straight for the ground below

Stronger than steel
Taller than the redwoods
His walls are forged of heartbreak
Betrayal
And tears
They desperately guard his calloused
bruised
and broken heart

Seemingly impenetrable
Unassailable
Yet slivers of light
filter through the cracks
Almost indiscernible

Almost

And so she sits
On the ground below

Within shooting distance
But unthreatening

And she waits

Waits for him to unload his bow
And place it at his feet
To set down his quiver

And meet her at the door

when the smoke clears

distance and time
clear the smoke from your eyes
in a way nothing else can

the most intense emotions
feel confusingly similar
when your heart and soul
are drowning in them

passion and desperation
have the same ache

longing and fear
leave the same empty pit

love and hate
boil inside with the same ferocity

passion and anger
burn the same in your soul

and only looking from a distance
can you finally see
that the peace you felt
when they laid beside you

was actually solace
from the constant worry
you felt while he was gone

and the comfort you find in his arms
is really exhaustion from
the silent battle
between your heart and your mind

the reality is
when the smoke clears
you often find you have to choose
between letting him love you
or loving yourself

barely sixteen

barely sixteen
she trembled as she waited
to see one pink line or two

and i think you know
how the story goes
when the answer was finally revealed

in a whirlwind of chaos
fear and shame
she changed her fate that day

she wouldn't be
who they said she'd be
she wouldn't fulfill
their judgmental prophecies
she wouldn't tell a soul

and nearly as quickly
as she had learned
she carried that promise
she ended it

but it wasn't over
not for her

as the days grew into weeks
and months
her heart ached
and her soul cried out

but she buried her pain
she stifled the tears
and didn't tell a soul

but hers knew

she would never be the same
like an eraser
on a heavy handed pencil mark
the imprint remained

a painful reminder
of what could have been
what should have been?

for twenty years
she carried shame in her heart
and phantom pain
in her empty womb
angry at the version of herself
who gave up
before she had even started

barely sixteen

that girl was barely sixteen
afraid
alone
ambushed
by a life she never envisioned

she hadn't known
just what she was giving up
how could she
just child herself

forgiveness comes in many forms
and sometimes
it's a gift you give yourself

forgiveness for the girl
who couldn't see a way out
who made a decision that would change them
forever

my darling girl
you did the best you could
for a girl of barely sixteen

Silver

As I dry her hair
I watch in wonder
As the dark gray strands
Turn silver between my fingers
I see her head bow just a bit
As she allows this to feel like pampering
Instead of helplessness

She's prideful
And fiercely independent
Frustrated by the toll
The years have taken on her body

I see the uncertainty in her eyes
And hear the exasperation in her voice
When her hands won't do
What they've always done
Or her body won't move
Like it always has

In these moments
I dry her hair a little longer
Her eyes closed
Perhaps imagining a simpler time
When this was something she chose

Rather than something she needed

I give her a few extra moments
To go back in time
Before her body and mind
Betrayed her

And for a few quiet moments
We both
Revel in her momentary solace

i got you

in the harsh light of the emergency room
she searches his face
for answers

his words betray his heart
afraid to let her in
afraid to need someone

unable to see his fear
but knowing it's just beneath the surface
she squeezes his hand and whispers

i got you

the answers came
not the ones they wanted
but the ones they feared

his face grew pale
his eyes avoiding hers
she leans in close and reminds him

i got you

she wakes in the night

to find the bed empty
and finds him alone in the kitchen

she pulls him close
and as he lays his head on her shoulder
she reminds him

i got you

she watches, helplessly
as they wheel the sterile bed down the long
hallway
and silently prays that he knows

i got you

in the middle of a restless night
he wraps his arms around her, pulling her into
him
and she knows that he knows

i got you

no matter the story
no matter the time
no matter the storm

i got you

Haunted

Not all houses are haunted
by the dead
Yes, sometimes spirits linger
in the last place that felt like home
Or roam the gardens
that felt like heaven
Or walk the halls that felt like hell

But sometimes
the rooms are haunted, instead
by promises unkept
dreams unfulfilled
or lifelong loves, divided

Sometimes the echo you hear
is the laughter of the children
so desperately wanted
but never realized

And the pacing steps you hear
down the hallway
are just the memory
of her footsteps
wondering if he's coming home

Sometimes the music
that echoes in the night
is just the song that played
when he buried his wife
too soon

and the chill in the air
is the chill of her heart
and the coldness
of her brutal revenge
for every bruise
every hateful word
and every broken bone

yes, sometimes the spirit stays behind
but often just the memories
are palpable in the air

no, houses are not always haunted
by the dead

to love and be loved

every now and then
when the sun has long since set
and their faces are hidden
deep within the shadows of the night
his heart reaches out to her
asking if it's safe

to speak
to feel
to let her in

while silently pleading with her

begging her to pretend
she cannot see it

and so she simply listens
getting lost in the words
that roll of his tongue
under the cover of darkness

she says very little
often nothing
afraid to startle his wounded heart
afraid it will retreat

back into the bunker
he built to protect it

she feels it
in the way he reaches for her
when he's fast asleep
pulls her in close
and sighs

she hears it
in the way he says her name
or asks how she slept
or if she's eaten today

she sees it
in those rare moments
when his guard slips down
and the truth in his eyes
betrays the walls he built

because despite his fear
the one thing he wants
the most in this life
is to share his heart again

freely
safely
completely

and his one desire is simply this

to love
and be loved

but the fear is so strong
the pain so raw
the hurt so deep
that it terrifies him to see

that he already does
and he already is

What I Know

If I've learned anything about love
in the last forty years
it's that I know nothing about love

I know about lust
And passion
And more than a little bit
about codependence

I know how to love

Deeply
Completely
Unconditionally

But I cannot fathom
what it feels like to be loved
the same way

Without reservation
Without hesitation

Fully
Passionately
Endlessly

Without footnotes

Or an asterisk

The Last Time

If I'd known that time was the last time,
I'd have rocked that little baby just a few
moments longer.
Held him a few more moments.
Read him one more story.

If I'd known that time was the last time,
I'd have pushed her one more time on the
swings,
played in the sandbox one more time,
built one more snowman.

If I'd known that time was the last time,
I'd have held her hand a little longer,
braided her hair one more time,
watched her favorite movie just once more.

If I'd known that time was the last time,
I'd have thrown the ball a few more times,
played with dolls a little longer,
colored one more page.

If I'd known that time was the last time,
I'd have held that hug at school at little longer,
played that game with him again,

the one I never understood.

If I'd known that time was the last time,
I'd have watched every second of that baseball
game,
taken a hundred more photos,
cheered so much louder.

But then again,
I always really knew
it might be the last time
didn't I?

the problem

the problem wasn't that she didn't know him
she knew him exactly
precisely
perfectly
the way he had intended
the problem was he didn't know himself

the problem wasn't that he wasn't sorry
he apologized a hundred times
a thousand?
two thousand?
he always said the words
the problem was that he never truly felt remorse

the problem wasn't that he didn't love her
he loved her completely
thoroughly
deeply
at least he thought he did
the problem was he never understood love

the problem wasn't that he walked away
or that he left abruptly
unapologetically
loudly

without even a moments hesitation
the problem was that he never looked back

until it was too late

her

mere moments after her arrival
I heard her cry for the first time
and my heart ached
like nothing I'd ever known
instantly, overwhelmingly
i realized

she needs me

her bouncing brown curls
disappeared from view
as she fell to the ground
her body bleeding
her spirit bruised
i wrapped my arms around her, knowing

she still needs me

her teenage heart is breaking
feeling love slip away
for the very first time
i know what she doesn't
this won't be the last time
but i say nothing
as she lays her head in my lap

i just take comfort in knowing

she still needs me

it's one am and the phone rings
my daughter's face lighting up the screen
she's crying
she's scared
we talk for hours
and as the tears turns to laughs
and the moonlight to a crimson glow
i've never been so sure

she still needs me

it's three am and i can't sleep
thoughts racing
i toss and turn on my tear stained pillow
as i reach for my phone
i see that she's awake too
and my heart sighs heavily in relief
and in that moment i realize

i need her too

I see it too

I see it too
The million ways
this could destroy us

The way this glass house we've built could
shatter
leaving us to bleed out on the floor
while we curse
I told you so's
at each other

I hear the deafening silence
of our laughter fading away
or even worse
replaced with angry vitriol
and hate filled gazes
thrown like daggers across the room

I feel the way you could slip away
leaving a eternal hole in me
that's shaped
like you

But I also see
what you're afraid to

I see the way the glass turns to steel

Impenetrable
Eternal
Unassailable

I hear the endless nights
of breathless laughter
and the mornings we're unceasingly awed
watching the cream swirl around
in my coffee
through your favorite glass mug

the one you always save for me

I see the way you never tire
of watching me dance in the kitchen
to a song you've heard a million times
and the way I stop and sing
my favorite part to you
every time

I see decades of eye rolls
and subtle jealous glances
thrown our way
because we're laughing
in grocery store aisles
and convenience store lines
but also in our darkest moments

in funeral home parking lots
and emergency rooms

I see the sideways grin you try to contain
when I tell you I got stuck in my sweater
or I can't find my keys
or my shirt is on inside out

again

I see the Christmas tree
now eight feet tall
every branch hanging low
weighed down with memories
stories
and inside jokes
that no one else could ever understand

I feel us at the end

Hands tightly clasped

Bodies intertwined

Hearts so tightly bound
they beat in sync

Oh, my darling
I see that, too

It Was(n't) Meant to Be

I never meant
to fall in love
with every single part of you

I never meant
to see the way your eyes light up
when you talk about your children
or fall in love with the way
you love them more than yourself

I never meant
to adore the way
you try to hide your smile
and pretend to be mad
when I beat you at cards
again

I never meant
to memorize
the callouses on your hands
or the lines around your eyes
that deepen when you laugh

I never meant
    to find comfort
        in feeling your chest rise and fall
            under my head
                as you drift off to sleep

I never meant
    to melt
        when I hear you say my name
            or when I hear your voice
                on the other end of the phone

I never meant
    for any of this to happen
        but as time goes by I'm realizing
            that just because we never meant for this
to happen
                doesn't mean

It wasn't meant to be

Don't Get Old

Don't get old

She tells me this every day
between heavy sighs
and long pauses
as she reaches into the depths of her mind
searching for the answers she knows are there

Or at least they used to be

I'm sorry

She says
when she can't remember how
to button her shirt
to put on her socks
or tie her shoes

Use it or lose it

She says
for the third time today
And as I watch her struggle
I resist every urge to help
without her request

because she's fiercely independent
and I will not be the one
to take that from her

Not after she's already lost
so much

I'm sorry it takes me so long

She says
So apologetically
that it breaks my heart
a little bit every time
because she feels like burden

Instead of a treasure

Could you help me?

She asks in exasperation
with defeat on her face
and a sadness in her eyes
I cannot comprehend

And never wish to

Thank you

She says wistfully

as she grasps my hand
followed by the words
that break my heart every time
Because I know
there's only one alternative

Don't get old